**Jokes for the Imbecile** by Mark Funnn and Will Funnn
Written by Imbeciles for Imbeciles

Interior Design by Mark Funnn and Will Funnn
Cover Design by Mark Funnn and Will Funnn
Edited by Sherri Funnn
Cover Photography by vitalytitov/Bigstock.com
Book Photography by Gudella/Bigstock.com, JanMika/Bigstock.com, Elnur/Bigstock.com, olly2/Bigstock.com, outsiderzone/Bigstock.com, Otna Ydur/Bigstock.com, zveiger/Bigstock.com, pzAxe/Bigstock.com, maxriesgo/Bigstock.com, soupstock/Bigstock.com, Rangizzz/Bigstock.com, bKletr/Bigstock.com, RetroClipArt/Bigstock.com
Published by FunnnBooks
**www.FunnnBooks.com**

**FunnnBooks**

ISBN-10: 0692342680
ISBN-13: 978-0-692-34268-8
Library of Congress Control Number: 2014922788
10 9 8 7 6 5 4 3 2 1  First Edition
BISAC1: HUMOR / Form / Jokes & Riddles
BISAC2: HUMOR / Form / Pictorial
BISAC3: JUVENILE FICTION / Humorous Stories
Printed in Pittsburgh, PA, United States of America

# Jokes for the Imbecile

## Written by Imbeciles for Imbeciles

By Mark & Will Funnn

Published by

FunnnBooks

# This Book Belongs To

_____

(Write your name here, Imbecile.)

# Contents

# FORWARD

Well, well, well. So, you bought a book that explicitly calls you an Imbecile! Don't worry and please be assured that you most certainly are — but we are too. The first book of its kind — showcasing the height of stupidity — was written by Imbeciles for Imbeciles. It is something that we are very proud of. We firmly believe that some Imbecile exists in everyone, big or small.

This Funnn book is meant to bring laughs and smiles in such a dark world that we live in... But, if after reading it you don't think so, that's ok. See if we care!

- M.F. & W.F.

# Chapter One:
# NURSERY RhyMES
## FOR THE iMBECiLE

## Tough Day for Dumpty

Humpty Dumpty sat on a wall
Humpty Dumpty had a great fall
All the King's Horses
Trampled him into the Ground
Oh, what a Bad Day that was

## No Wonder i Hate Peas!

Pease Porridge Hot
Pease Porridge Cold
Pease Porridge Warm
Pease Porridge Skunked

## Time to Diet, Muffet

"Little" Miss Muffet
Ate in front of the TV
And Wheyed 700 pounds

## Peter Piper Peck

Peter Piper Peck
Peppered a Particular Pickle
Or did he Pickle a Particular Pepper?
No clue.

## Something's Out There

Star Man, Star Face
First Star Man Face I see tonight
I wish I May, I wish I Might
Blast you with my evil Death Ray tomorrow night

## Stinky Feet

There was an old woman who lived in a shoe
That smelled so badly
She didn't know what to do
So, she bought foot spray and sprayed the whole house
Too bad the foot spray was Toxic

## Leap for the Stars

Hey Diddle Diddle
The Cat and the fiddle
The cow jumped over the Moon
The little dog laughed
To see such a sight:
A Martian eating the Cow's Brain

## Boy, That's a Shame...

Little Boy Blue
Was never Revived
Sadly

## Jump Jack, Jump!

Jack wasn't Nimble
Jack wasn't Quick
Jack has 3rd Degree Burns

## Love at First Disaster

Old Mother Hubbard
Sat in a cupboard next to a Skeleton Man
The cupboard crashed down to the floor like a Bomb
And she became his Wife

## "REGULAR" KING COLE

Old King Cole
Was a merry old sole
And a merry old sole was he
He called for his pipe
And he Puked in his bowl
And he called for his Stool Softener

## LUCKY MOUSE

Hickory Dickory Dakery Dock
The mouse ran into the side of the Clock
The Clock came down
With a very loud Crash
Luckily, he only lost one Ear

## SLEEPY PIG

This little Piggy went to market
This little Piggy stayed home
This little Piggy never woke up

## CUTE LITTLE LAMMIE

Mary had a little Lamb
Its face was White as Yellow Snow
And everywhere that Mary went
The Lamb was sure to Stink
Badly

# Chapter Two:
# Colors
## for the imbecile

Q: What do you get when you mix Yellow with Yellow?
A: SUPER Yellow

Q: What is Red, Orange, Yellow, Green, Blue, Indigo, and Violet?
A: A bunch of random colors

Q: What is Green, Blue, and Red?
A: Some colors in a Rainbow

Q: How do you tell two colors apart?
A: Look at them closely and think it through. Take as much time as you need to get it right. If this doesn't work, the human race may not be right for you.

Q: How many colors are in a computer?
A: As many as the naked eye can imagine

Q: What color is a Pink flamingo's crap?
A: Brown

Q: How is Blue Cheese made?
A: You mix a bacteria called Penicillium with the color Blue

Q: What's the Yellowist thing in the Solar System?
A: The color Yellow

Q: What's Black, Gray, and Yellow?
A: Beans

Q: What's Blue, Gray, and White?
A: Rice

Q: What rare Bird is Orange in color?
A: The Orange Jay

Q: What is the Greenist thing on the entire Earth?
A: The color Green

Q: What beautifully covers 75% of the Earth's surface?
A: The color Blue

Q: What's the White part of the eye known as?
A: The Eye-White

Q: What happened to the Blue Elephant among all the Gray ones?
A: The Poacher shot him first

# Chapter Three:
# Science
## for the imbecile

Q: What are the Three R's of Stupidity?
A: Reeking, Rotting & Rooster Tick

Q: What is the tastiest thing in SouthWestern Louisiana?
A: Taste

Q: What is the absolute heaviest thing on Earth?
A: Weight

Q: What is the fastest object in the Universe?
A: Speed

Q: What did the Sky say to Outer Space?
A: Get a Life, SpaceNut

Q: How many Sugar Cubes can safely be eaten during one sitting?
A: 1000 (Caution: Eating 1001 will cause sudden Death)

Q: What is the furthest distance recorded in human history?
A: Length

Q: What is the most savory smell found in a Bakery?
A: Scent

# Chapter Four: Songs

## for the imbecile

## Goodbye

Row, Row, Row Your Boat
Gently Down the Abyss
Merrily, Merrily, Merrily, Merrily
You are going to be Missed

## Shoo Fly

Shoo Fly, don't bother me
Oh Fly, You smell like pee
Shoo Fly, don't bother me
My Master is a Dunce

## Extermination!

Three Blind Mice, Three Blind Mice
Their tails were chopped off by the Farmer's Wife
Have you ever seen that much Blood in your Life?
As Three Blind Mice...Horribly Killed

## Poison Tar

Twinkle Twinkle Little piece of Tar
How you smell like Poison Gas
On the road, you are so Black
So we can drive to our house and Back
Twinkle Twinkle Little piece of Tar
How you smell like Poison Gas

# Chapter Five:
# Poems
## for the imbecile

## APPLE BUTTER

Apple Butter, Apple Butter, I hate you
Apple Butter, Apple Butter, you taste like Poo
Apple Butter, Apple Butter, oh me oh my
Apple Butter, Apple Butter, I hope you Die!

## PURPLE

Roses are Red
Violets are Purple
Oh, crap!
Nothing rhymes with Purple

## BAD POEM

Poem, Poem
You rhyme with: O-M
Poem, Poem
You're not very good.  Seriously.
But, you bring a smile to my heart anyway

## FOOL

Jimmy Jimmy Kembo
Jimmy Jimmy Kempo
Kempo Kempo Kembo
Charlie Charlie Chunko

# Chapter Six:
# Recipes
## for the imbecile

## Moose-Beer

| | |
|---|---|
| Happy Ingredients: | 1 cup of Root Beer |
| Sad Ingredients: | 1 chunk of Moose |
| Preparation: | Mix all ingredients in a Blender |
| Serving Suggestions: | Serve Cold with Ice (May induce Drool) |
| Nutritional Value: | 1 |

## Snoter

| | |
|---|---|
| Happy Ingredients: | 1 cup of Water |
| Sad Ingredients: | 1 cup of Snot |
| Preparation: | Mix all ingredients in a Blender |
| Serving Suggestions: | Serve heated in a Microwave for 10 seconds (Hold nose to avoid Vomiting) |
| Nutritional Value: | -2 |

## Hot-Cold Dogs

| | |
|---|---|
| Happy Ingredients: | 1 Hot Dog |
| Sad Ingredients: | 1 Dog Heart |
| Preparation: | Mix all ingredients in a Blender, Form into the shape of a Hot Dog |
| Serving Suggestions: | Serve chilled on a Hot Dog bun (Slight risk of Rabies) |
| Nutritional Value: | -5 |

## TURKEY JAM

| | |
|---|---|
| Happy Ingredients: | 1 Cup of Oats, 1 Cup of Sugar |
| Sad Ingredients: | 1 Turkey Gut |
| Preparation: | Mix all ingredients in a Blender |
| Serving Suggestions: | Refrigerate, Serve on warm Toast (Barf bag highly recommended) |
| Nutritional Value: | 4 |

## LAMBINADE

| | |
|---|---|
| Happy Ingredients: | 1 Cup of Milk, 1 Cup of Sugar |
| Sad Ingredients: | 3 Lamb Chunks |
| Preparation: | Mix all ingredients in a Blender |
| Serving Suggestions: | Serve Cold with Ice (Best when Lamb Chunks are fully blended) |
| Nutritional Value: | 0 |

## HORSi (PRONOUNCED: HORSE EYE) SAUCE

| | |
|---|---|
| Happy Ingredients: | 1 Cup of Sauce, 1 Radish |
| Sad Ingredients: | 1 Horse Eye |
| Preparation: | Mix all ingredients in a Blender |
| Serving Suggestions: | Serve on Crackers or Rice Cakes (It's not fun chewing on the Eye, otherwise good) |
| Nutritional Value: | -0 |

# Chapter Seven:
# Periodic Chart
## for the imbecile

The Periodic Chart for the Imbecile is carefully maintained by the American Academy of the Abomination Arts & Crafts (AAAAC). The Elements listed here can be used for your day-to-day living and are in-use today by most Imbeciles Earthwide.

# PERIODIC CHART FOR THE IMBECILE

| Ab | Bbs | C | D |
|---|---|---|---|
| Absolute bozo | Bee Bee Sole | Chum | Dander |
| **E** | **F** | **G** | **Hg** |
| Earwax | Iron | Greens | Hot Dog |
| **I** | **J** | **Kc** | **Li** |
| Ice Chips | Junk | Kettle Corn | Liquid |
| **M** | **m** | **Nl** | **O** |
| Moon | little moon | Numbskull | Onion Ring |
| **Pb** | **Q** | **R** | **Si** |
| Po' Boy | Quicksand | Rocks | Science |
| **Ts** | **U** | **V** | **Wc** |
| Tube Sock | Unibrow | Velocity | Whoopee Cushion |
| **?** | **X** | **Yf** | **Zg** |
| Huh? | X-Ray Beams | Yellow Fizz | Zoo Gas |

# Chapter Eight:
# Tongue Twisters
## For the Imbecile

These tongue twisters are sure to bring decades of laughter to you and your entire extended family. Repeat each of them Twenty Five times. This can be done at your leisure, day or night. Good luck and many thanks!

## Wood Chunks

How much wood would a wood-chuck Puke, if a wood-chuck could Puke chunks?

## Classic Twist

Tongue Twister Tongue – Twister Tongue Twister

## Canker

Klinko Klinko Kink Canker Klop

## Chicken Twist

Baak – Baak – Block – Baak
(HINT: A Chicken makes this sound: "Baak")

## Help!

S.O.S . O.S.O.  O.O.O.  S.
(HINT: This is Morse Code for: "Help, I'm an Idiot!")

## Black Twist

Black – Black – Back – Black

# Chapter Nine:
# Holiday Colors
## For the Imbecile

**Q:** What's Brown and White on New Year's Day?
**A:** Baby New Year's Dirty Diaper

**Q:** What's Red on Valentine's Day?
**A:** A Rejected Valentine floating down the River

**Q:** What's Green on Saint Patrick's Day?
**A:** The Leprechaun's head on a Stick

**Q:** What's Black on Arbor Day?
**A:** Ashes after the Forest Fire

**Q:** What's Pink at Easter time?
**A:** The Easter Bunny's Conjunctivitis

**Q:** What's Red, White, and Blue on the 4th of July?
**A:** Sinew, Bone, and Veins found after the Fireworks Accident

**Q:** What's Yellow on Columbus Day?
**A:** Christopher's ripe Pimple

**Q:** What's Orange on Halloween?
**A:** The Pumpkin's rotting Brain

**Q:** What's Brown on Thanksgiving?
**A:** The Pilgrim's ugly Mole

**Q:** What's Red at Christmas time?
**A:** Santa's Chapped Buttocks after his long Sleigh Ride

# ABOUT THE AUTHORS

Mark and Will Funnn live in a wonderful neighborhood on Earth. It's a place where the sky can be seen for miles and miles on end. They enjoy watching for ducks and/or bats roaming these very skies.

Oftentimes, they enjoy eating Funnn foods and sipping drinks on their back porch while lifting weights or playing banjo and such. These two embody the core principles of being a total Imbecile: Thinking, Smelling, and Breathing like an Imbecile at all times. This cannot be denied — if only for a moment or two. Good day. All the best. You have our condolences. And above all: Thanks for being an Imbecile like us! - M.F. & W.F.

## Funnn Facts about the Funnns:

| Favorite | MARK | WILL |
|---|---|---|
| Favorite Smell: | Fresh Scent | Raw Sewage |
| Favorite Planet: | Earth | Earth |
| Favorite Moon: | Earth's Moon | Calypso |
| Favorite Allergy: | Dairy | Peanut |
| Favorite Disease: | TapeWorm | Scurvy |
| Favorite Organ: | Cochlea | Islets of Langerhans |
| Favorite Snack: | Meat Spread (Any Variety) | Crust |
| Favorite Element: | Absolute bozo (Ab) | Velocity (V) |
| Favorite Dessert: | Egg Pie | Sugar Cubes |
| Favorite Scab Spot: | Knee | Elbow |
| Favorite Color: | Purple | Green |

CPSIA information can be obtained at www.ICGtesting.com
Printed in the USA
BVOW07s0743271215

431006BV00004B/4/P

9 780692 342688